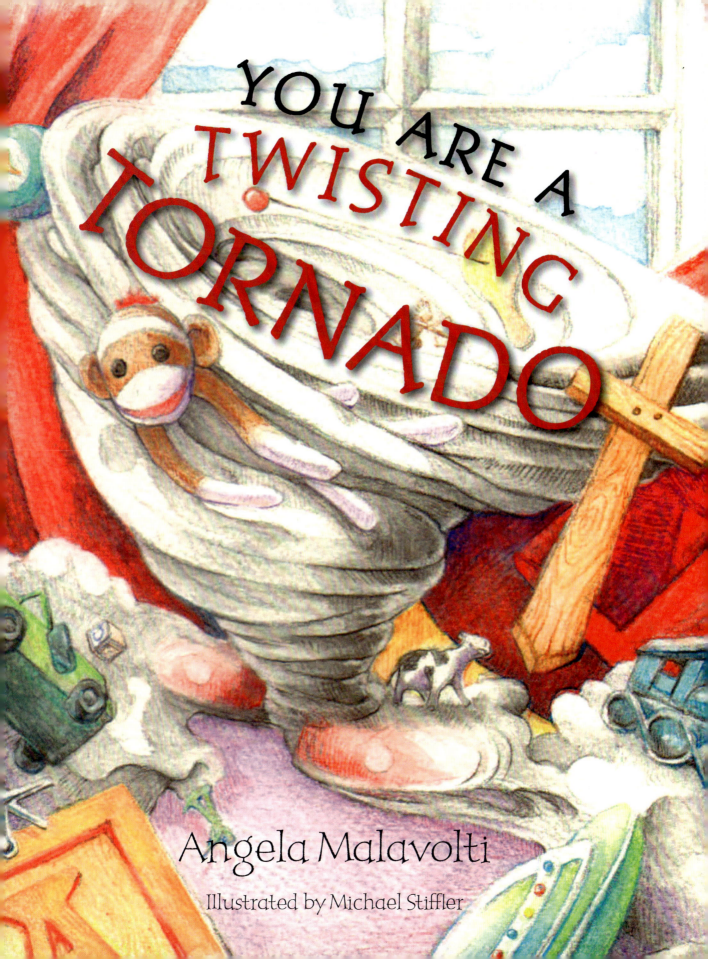

Copyright © 2011 by Angela Malavolti

Illustrations by Michael Stiffler

Published by Jungle Wagon Press
Rockford, IL 61101

All Rights Reserved.
No portion of this publication may be copied,
transmitted, posted, duplicated or otherwise used
without the express written approval of the publisher.

ISBN: 978-0-9834092-0-5

CPSIA Compliance Information: Batch 0511
For further information contact
RJ Communications
Phone 800 621-2556

Printed in the USA

"For Sammy, my twisting "tomato."
-A.M.

"For those who believe..."
-M.S.

You are a twisting tornado;
you leave a path behind you.

You are a puffy white cloud;
I'm delighted when I find you.

You are early morning fog—
to me, so tightly clinging.

Your voice, it wakes the sunshine
like the birds of springtime singing.

You are a meteor shower;
You put on quite a show.

You're the sound of children laughing
as they play in fluffy snow.

One moment, you are gentle breeze,
then suddenly—a squall.

Like an unexpected rainstorm
your giant teardrops fall.

Your temper is like lightning;
who knows when it will strike!

But when you smile, peace abounds
as on a clear and starry night.

And when it's time for quiet,
you are hail-balls pelting.

Then after hours of playing,
you are an icicle melting.

You dream just like thunder:
rolling, crashing, turning-

yet you wake up with more energy
than the hot July Sun burning.

Your laughter is volcanic:
boisterous and heaping.

The calm eye of a hurricane
passes by me when you're sleeping.

You, my child, are perfect
in every kind of weather.
No matter what the forecast-
my love is yours forever.

FUN FACT FORECAST

SUNSHINE
The Sun is the closest star to Earth. It is a giant ball of burning gas and energy. If the Earth were as small as a pea, the Sun would be as big as a beach ball!

METEOR SHOWER
A meteor is a rock that zooms into Earth's atmosphere from outer space. A meteor looks like a bright star shooting across the sky. A meteor shower occurs when many meteors fall on the same night. If you look closely, you might find a meteorite in your own back yard!

SNOW
The largest snowflake ever found was bigger than this book!

RAIN CLOUDS
A rain cloud is a collection of tiny drops of water in the sky. When it becomes heavy enough, it pours the water droplets down as rain.

FUN FACT FORECAST

LIGHTNING
Lightning is a powerful flow of electricity between a cloud and the ground.

FOG
Have you ever wondered what it would be like to touch a cloud? Go outside on a foggy day and you'll be standing in a cloud! Fog usually forms when water droplets evaporate from a river, lake, pond, or puddle.

HURRICANE
Although hurricane winds and storms are strong enough to destroy cities, the weather in the center, or eye, is usually very calm and peaceful.

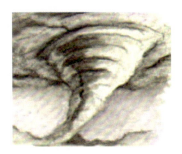

TORNADO
When a tornado is approaching, it often sounds like a loud train. The safest place to be in a tornado is in your basement.

ABOUT THE AUTHOR

Angela Malavolti's love of writing is second only to her love of family. *You Are a Twisting Tornado* was inspired by her energetic three-year-old son whose temperament changes unexpectedly from blue sky to tornado... much like the weather in the Midwest where she resides happily with her husband and two children.